Living in the Best Homes

Written by
Jill Atkins

Ransom

Animals make their homes in lots of odd sites.

This fox has made a home at the side of a ditch. A fox's home is sometimes called a **den**.

These rabbits have made a new home inside a log, under the ground.

Some pet rabbits have their home in a hutch.

It's not good for rabbits to dwell in a little hutch. They need a bigger home, with room to run around.

This donkey goes to sleep at night in a shed.

This dog might sleep in a kennel.

This home has a thatched roof. The thatch is made of long stems of straw.

Pests such as rats, squirrels or bugs can make their home in the thatch.

People do not like this! The pests can spoil the thatch.

A lot of bugs make their home in the garden.

Gardeners do not like some of these bugs.

They do not like caterpillars in their garden patch. The caterpillars eat the crops.

They do not like slugs or snails.

Slugs make their homes in damp corners of the garden.

Snails have their home on their back. They might eat the crops too.

Gardeners like bees.
Bees collect nectar from the flowers.

Bees have a home in a hive.

Joe, Laura and Paula looked for insects in a patch of ground. There were a few interesting things living there.

This is an earwig.

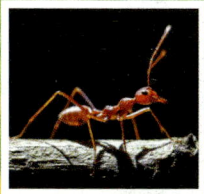

This is an ant.

Do you like this bug and insect home?

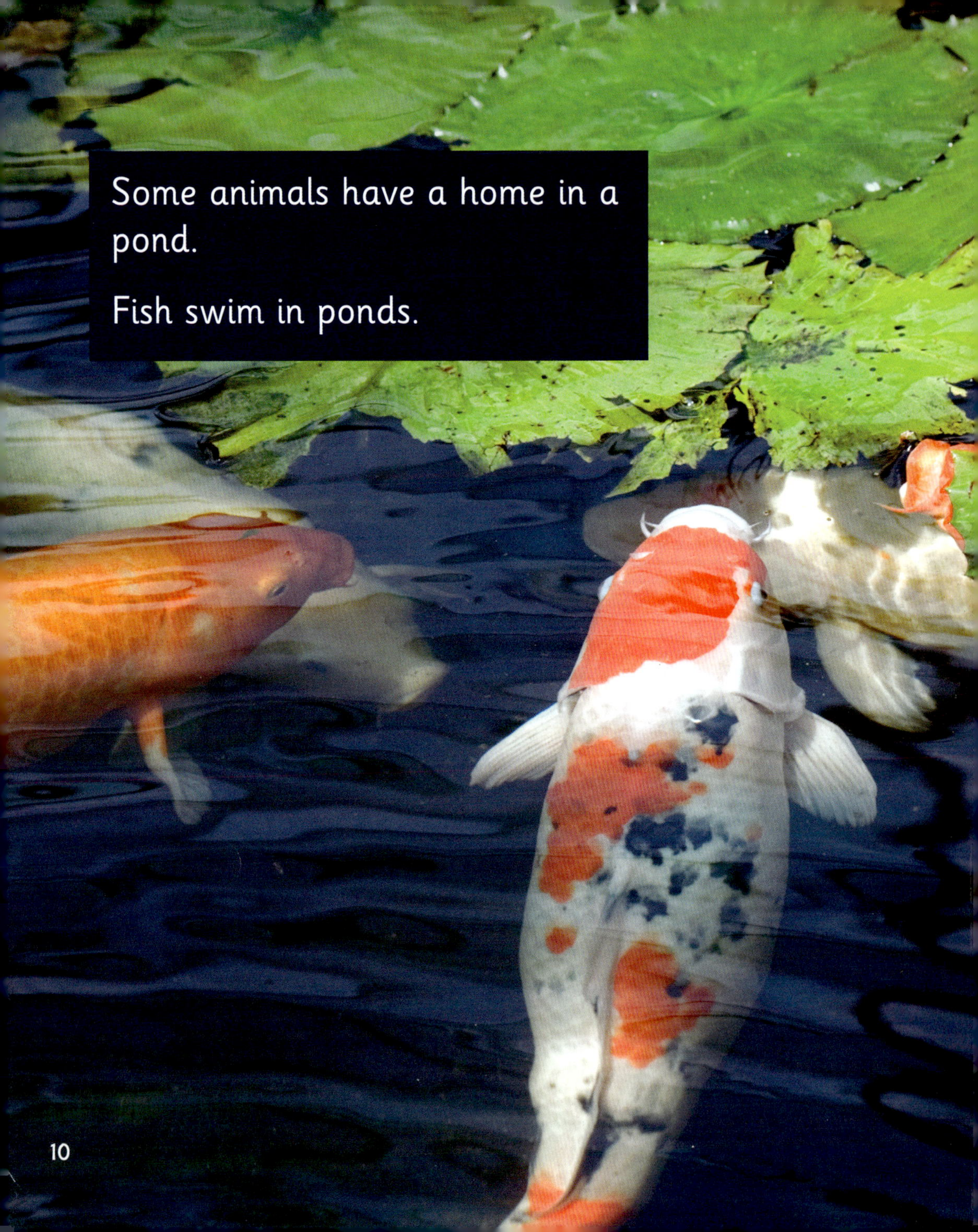

Some animals have a home in a pond.

Fish swim in ponds.

Frogs and toads have a home near a pond. In winter, their home is under a stone or a tree root.

In spring, they come to the pond to lay their eggs. The eggs are called frogspawn or toadspawn.

Ducks and coots often make a nest near a pond or a river. Their chicks will stay in the nest until they can swim.

Birds make a nest and lay their eggs there. The nest will be a home for their chicks until they can take flight.

Jackdaws like to make a nest on a chimney. It is their home.

Storks make their nests on chimneys too.

This is a swift's nest. The chicks are at home in the nest.

The swifts catch flies in their beaks to feed the chicks.

These bats sleep in a cave in the daytime. Then they go out at night.

They catch flies too.

Which animal has the best home?